# More
# Pants

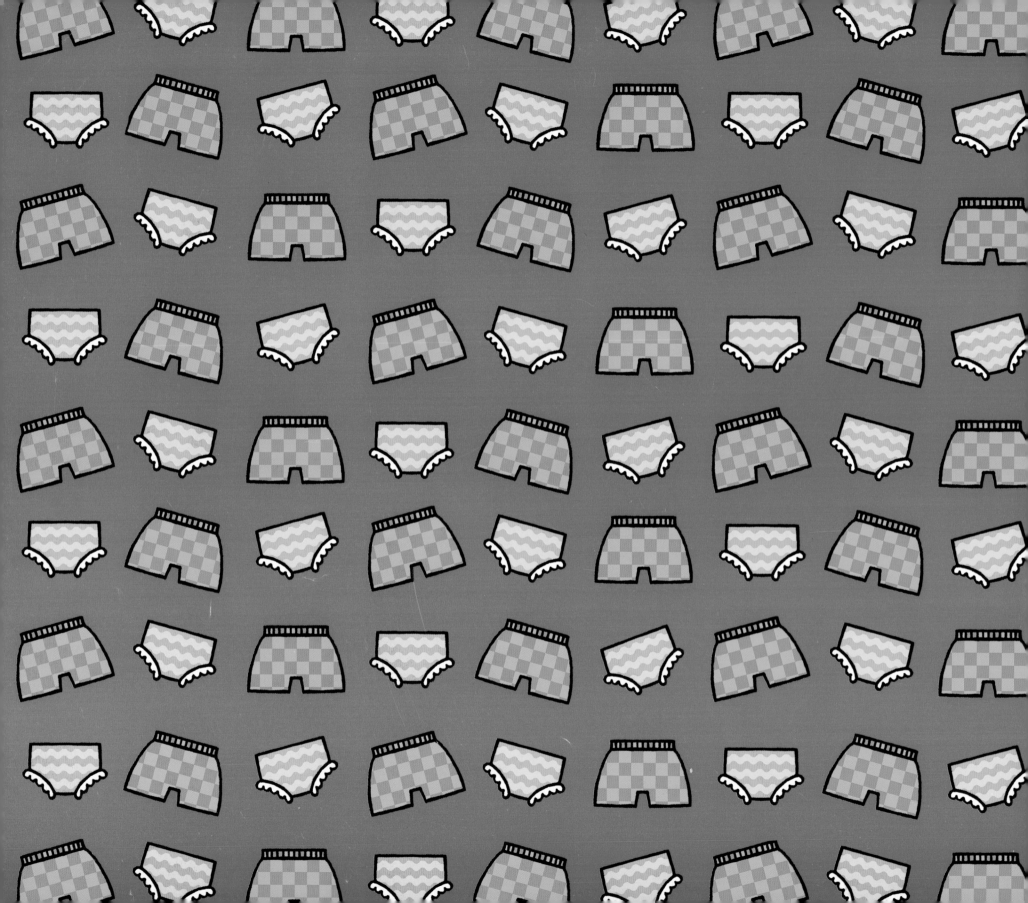

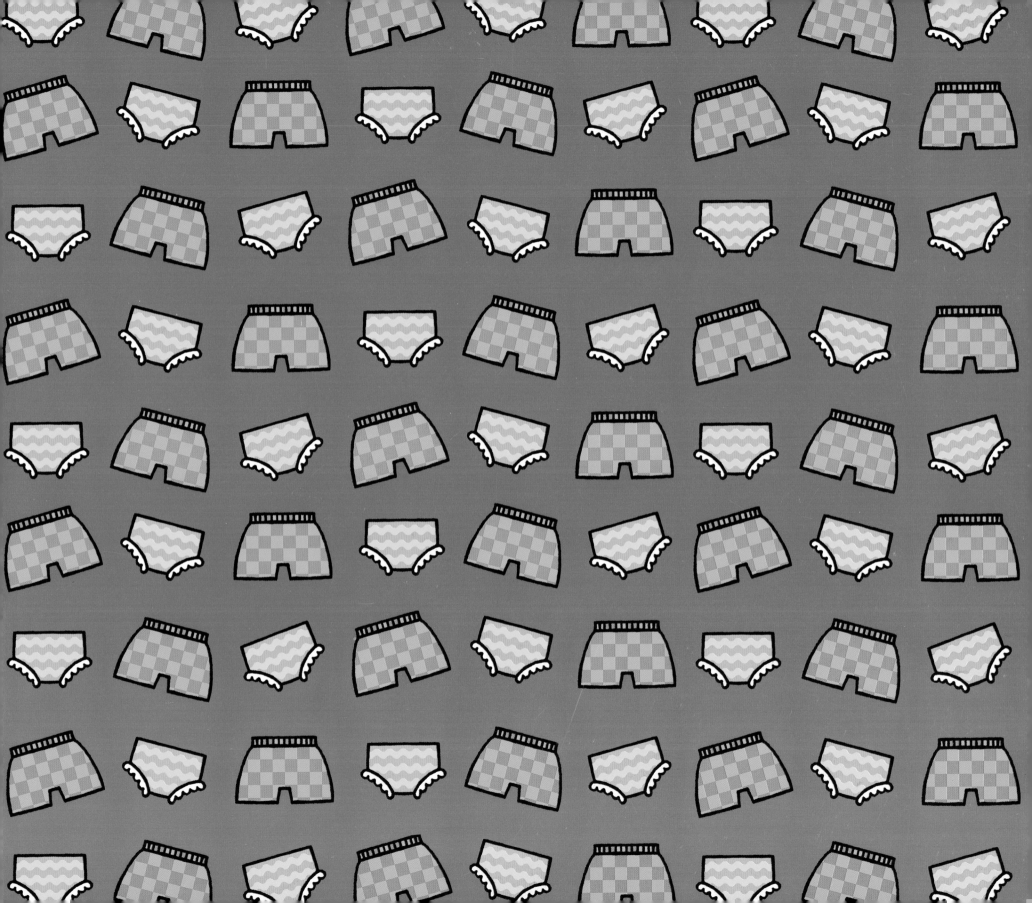

# For Jackson – G.A.
# For Pam, John, Maya and Sienna – N.S.

MORE PANTS
A PICTURE CORGI BOOK 978 0 552 57008 4

First published in Great Britain by David Fickling Books,
A division of Random House Children's Publishers UK
A Random House Group Company

David Fickling edition published 2007
Picture Corgi edition published 2008

Text copyright © Giles Andreae, 2007
Illustrations copyright © Nick Sharratt, 2007

Picture Corgi books are published by Random House Children's Publishers UK
61–63 Uxbridge Road, London W5 5SA

www.**randomhousechildrens**.co.uk

Addresses for companies within The Random House Group Limited
can be found at: www.randomhouse.co.uk/offices.htm

THE RANDOM HOUSE GROUP Limited Reg. No. 954009

A CIP catalogue record for this book is available from the British Library.

Printed in China

# More Pants

**Giles Andreae**

**Nick Sharratt**

PICTURE CORGI

Red pants, green pants

# Yellow submarine pants

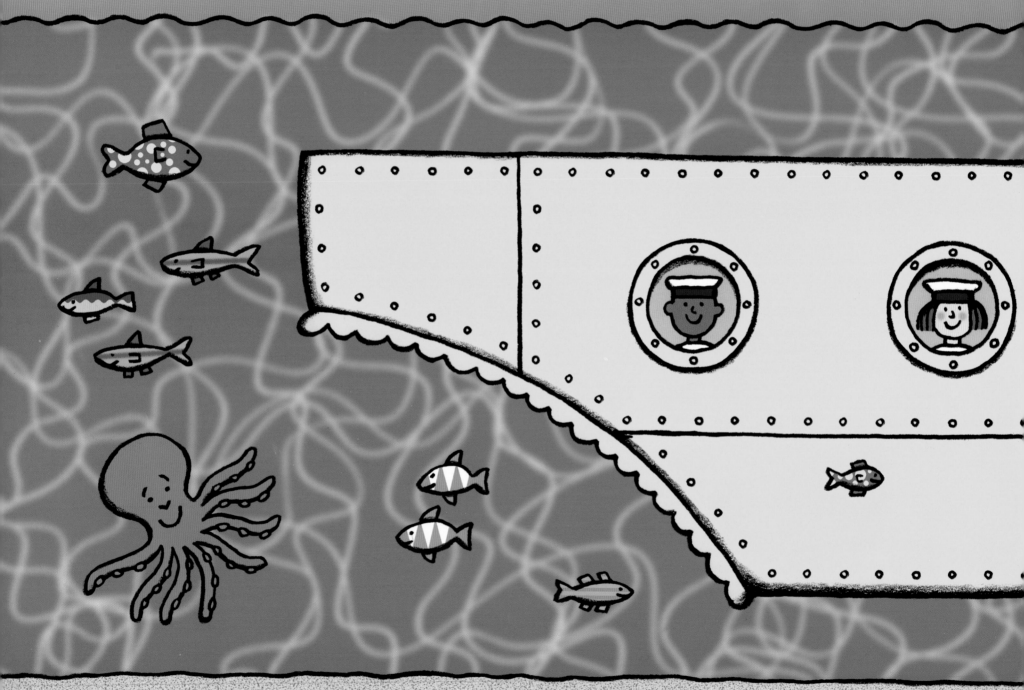

Tickling your tummy pants

And matching bra!

Arty pants,
party pants

Black belt in
karate pants

Have you done a farty pants?

Stretchy pants
for fitting an
extra-special
mate in

Puffy pants,
fluffy pants

Pants
for a
scary
dinosaur

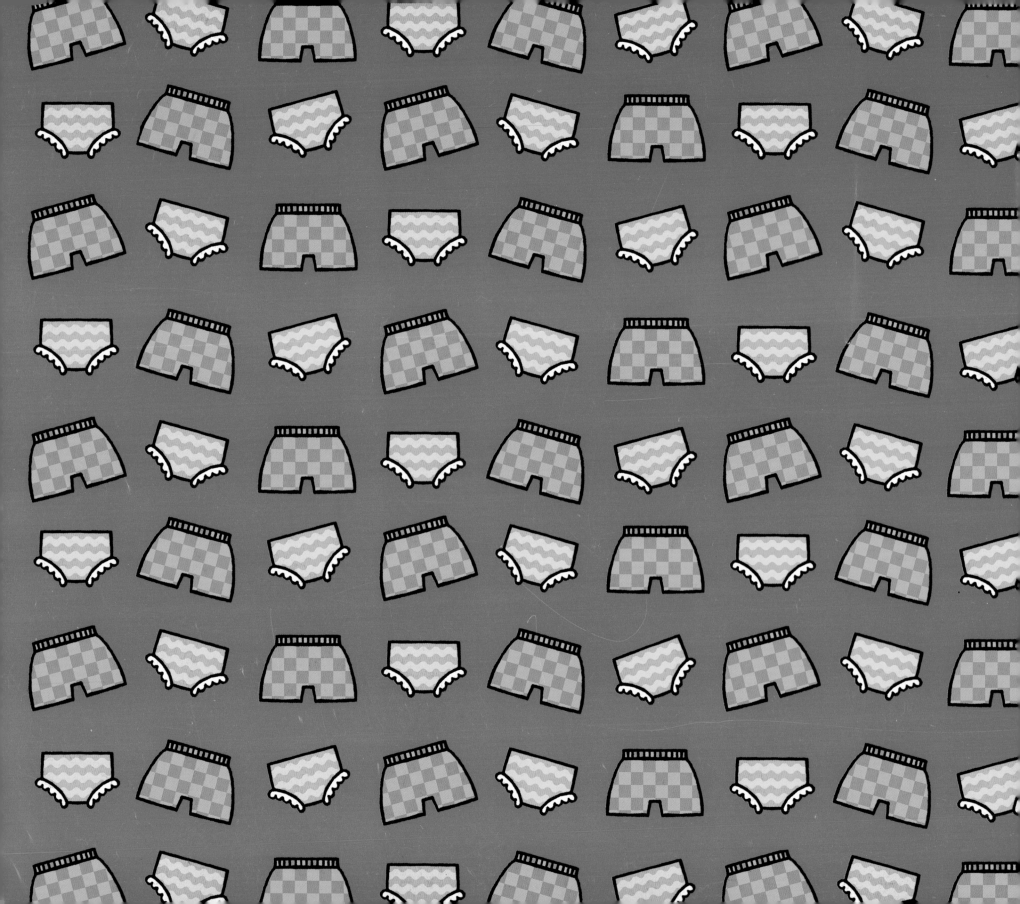

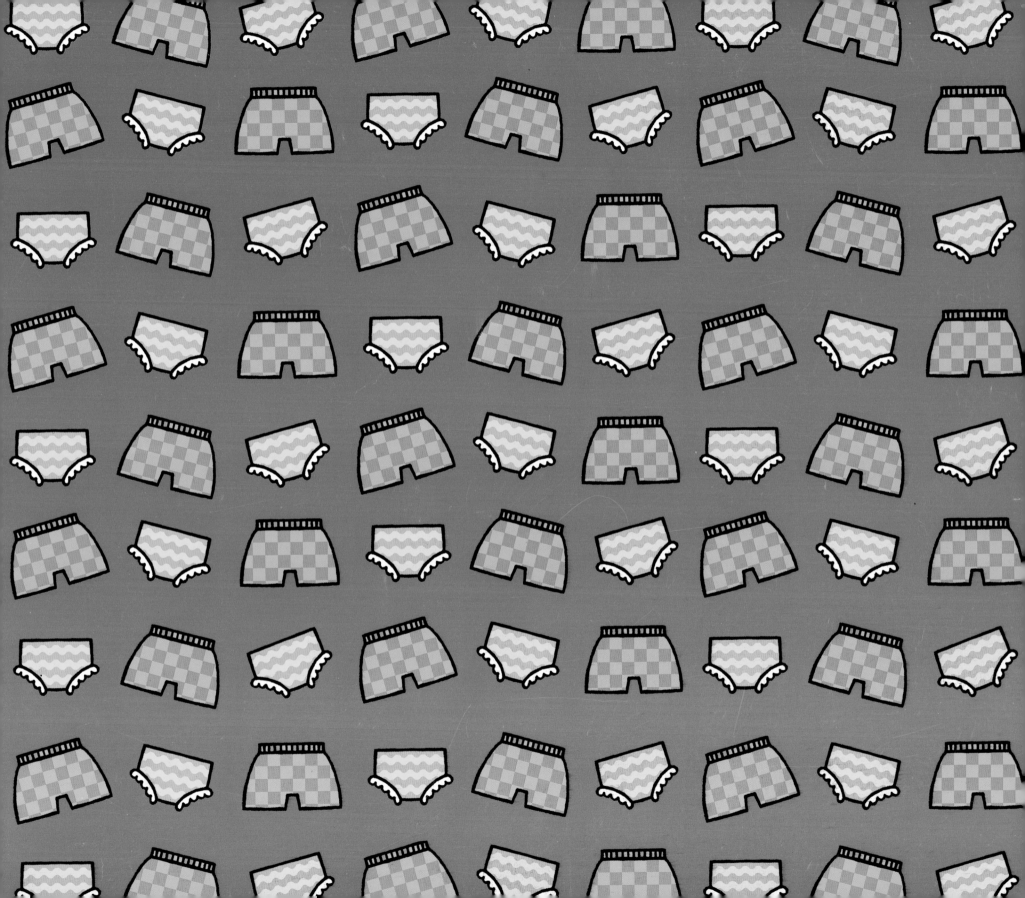